# THE STORY OF
# CRUEL AND UNUSUAL

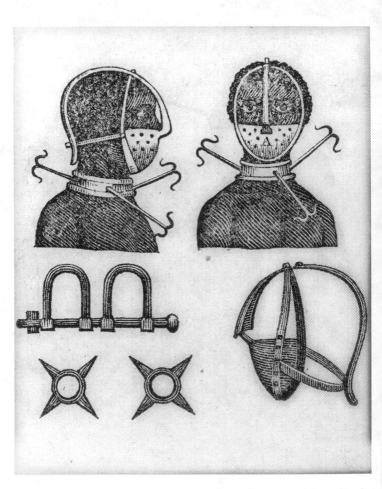

Implements used to restrain American slaves, from *The Penitential Tyrant* (1807), by Thomas Branagan. Courtesy of the Library of Congress.

# THE STORY OF CRUEL AND UNUSUAL

Colin Dayan

*Foreword by Jeremy Waldron*

A Boston Review Book

THE MIT PRESS  Cambridge, Mass.  London, England

This book was set in Adobe Garamond by *Boston Review*.

Designed by Joshua J. Friedman

Library of Congress Cataloging-in-Publication Data
Dayan, Joan.
    The story of cruel and unusual / Colin Dayan.
        p.   cm. — (Boston Review books)
    Includes bibliographical references.
    ISBN: 978-0-262-04239-0 (hardcover : alk. paper)
    ISBN: 978-0-262-55196-0 (paperback)
    1. Prisoners—Abuse of—United States—History.
2. Prisoners—Legal status, laws, etc.—United States.
3. Detention of persons—United States—History.
4. Torture—United States—History.  5. Prisoners of war—
United States.  I. Title.
HV9469.D39 2007
364.60973—dc22                              2006030290

*For David*

We read of death inflicted by hanging, beheading, burning, drowning, stoning, precipitation from rocks; we read of loss of ears, nose, upper-lip, hands and feet; we read of castration and flogging and sale into slavery … But the worst cruelties belong to a politer time.

Frederick Pollock and Frederic William Maitland, *The History of English Law* (1898)

# CONTENTS

FOREWORD  ix

1  Trials of definition  3
2  Codes of law, bodies of color  9
3  Dead to rights  17
4  Mental states  27
5  The threshold of suffering  39
6  Tools of terror  51
7  Torture language  59
8  A new legal regime?  73
9  Giving flesh to history  87

NOTES  93

*Jeremy Waldron*

# FOREWORD

THERE'S A SERIES OF STORIES WE TELL ourselves—one after the other—about the shameful use of torture by American soldiers and intelligence operatives in places whose names read now like a litany of national disgrace—Abu Ghraib in Iraq, the U.S. naval base at Guantánamo Bay, Cuba, and Bagram Airbase in Afghanistan. The stories are designed to condemn us, but also to reassure. We deplore the abuses that happened at these places, but we deplore them as a *lapse*—as a falling away from our normally high standards of respect for human rights, particularly the rights of the most despised and the most vulnerable.

In the first, very familiar story, we talk about a few rotten apples contaminating an otherwise scrupulously clean barrel— a few abusive lowlifes like Charles Graner and Lynndie England at Abu Ghraib who abused the prisoners assigned to their care (and did us the additional disservice of photographing the results). We are better than that, we say: those soldiers (reservists from the Appalachians—what do you expect?) were insufficiently trained and wrongly left unsupervised.

In a second story—a little more honest—we acknowledge that the nightmare at Abu Ghraib happened in part because professional U.S. government interrogators asked military police officers "to set favorable conditions" (that was the euphemism) for the interrogation of detainees. We acknowledge that the abuse began when Major General Geoffrey Miller moved to Abu Ghraib from Guantánamo Bay, where abusive methods (involving animals and sexual humiliation) were said to be achieving good results. And Miller was responding to a bad situation in Baghdad. Bombs were going off. Information was desperately needed. We tell ourselves that the deplorable use of these methods is understandable: good men, field officers and professional intelligence operatives faced with a confused and terrifying situation, will misjudge the tactics they may use to get it under control.

But that's not all. There is a third story to tell, about public servants, safe in Washington, in the Department of Justice, the White House, and the Department of Defense. These were the authors of the infamous "torture memos"—highly trained legal scholars, a future Ninth Circuit judge, a law professor on leave from Berkeley, a future attorney general of the United States—who in 2002 and 2003 set out to see if anything could be done to blur international, constitutional, and domestic law that seemed to put torture completely beyond the pale. They tried to restrict the application of the Geneva Conventions so that Taliban and al Qaeda captives would not be covered by minimum safeguards prohibiting "mutilation, cruel treatment and torture … [and] outrages upon personal dignity" against those who had laid down their arms.

Again, we say to ourselves that it was an outrage that intelligent young men educated in our best law schools and recruited to the public service should seek to subvert the law in this way. But we distance ourselves from this horror as well: had the Justice Department been manned by more honorable and less ideological lawyers in the months following 9/11, cooler and more appropriate legal advice would have emerged, more consonant with this country's moral traditions and its international obligations.

And then there's a fourth story we tell as a sort of background to all this, a story to explain why we—the storytellers—were for a few moments or a few years not entirely convinced in our own minds that torturing terrorists *was* utterly out of the question. We were angry and frightened after 9/11. Who knew what the next wave of attack would involve? A dirty bomb in Manhattan? Biological weapons in Washington, D.C.? We were not as resolute as we should have been in defense of basic rights. *Still*—we tell ourselves—this was an aberration. Had we not been terrorized, had we not become so enraged, the better angels of our nature might have prevailed.

And they might prevail still. With appropriate repentance and a new determination to uphold human rights, with better training for our reservists, less cynical politicians, and a lesser role for neoconservative lawyers from the Federalist Society in American government, the country might redeem the soul that we imperiled when we turned our backs on the part of our heritage that condemns cruelty on the part of the government and commands respect for the rights and dignity of everyone.

THOSE ARE THE STORIES WE TELL OURselves. But Colin Dayan comes perilously close to depriving us of even these meager crumbs of moral comfort. For Dayan has little patience with this dialectic of heritage and betrayal—the trouble, she says, is not the betrayal. It is the heritage.

We have a heritage in America of torture and brutality, first against slaves and secondly against prisoners. Far from representing the better angels of our nature, the U.S. Constitution was long ago condemned as "a covenant with death and an agreement with hell." We had legal codes that prohibited cruelty, but which (as Dayan shows) understood cruelty as *excessive* whipping and *unnecessary* biting or tearing with dogs. And when we abolished slavery, we did not abolish it unconditionally, but with the Thirteenth Amendment qualification that slavery is okay for prisoners: "Neither slavery nor involuntary servitude, except as a punishment for crime whereof the party shall have been duly convicted."

And that pretty much ensured that the qualifications in our understanding of cruelty necessary to maintain an effective system of enslavement would continue to distort the understanding of cruelty in the operation of our penal system. As Dayan argues, there is no long-established heritage of using the Eighth Amendment to protect the rights of those we hate and fear. On the contrary, there is a long tradition in our courts of limiting and narrowing its application.

And what did we think? The Eighth Amendment had to coexist for three generations with an institution that relied on force and violence to subjugate a racially distinguished population; our jurists became adept at finding ways of saying that "necessary" cruelty wasn't cruelty. Anything we hope for from the Eighth Amendment has to be understood against the background of those necessities.

Not only that, but Dayan demonstrates a sort of mean-spirited formalism in the recent application of the Eighth Amendment. The repetition of a failed execution in the electric chair is not cruel and unusual punishment; it is just as though the prisoner were executed after having been the victim of an accident, like a fire in his cell. Prisoners injured by their shackles are not being punished in a cruel fashion any more than "if the guard accidentally stepped on the prisoner's toe and broke it." When we were told in the "torture memos" that brutal interrogation methods could not be said to violate the Eighth Amendment because they were not inflicted as punishment—the camps at Guantánamo Bay are not penitentiaries, for heaven's sake!—this was not an aberration by a few neo-Straussian law professors. It was *business as usual* for Eighth Amendment jurisprudence.

IT IS, AS I HAVE SAID, A DEPRESSING story that Dayan has to tell, because it goes against the grain of what we want to tell ourselves: that we have a shining tradition of commitment to individual and minority rights; that our government is constitutionally prohibited from acting cruelly to its charges; that it represents the rule of laws, not men; and that such a government necessarily repudiates the idea of civil death and is committed to keeping alive the legal personality and basic rights of even its most hardened criminals. We in fact have a tradition of mocking the claim that all men are created equal. We have a tradition of "reading down" any constitutional limits on cruelty so that they restrain only the most sadistic and egregious acts. The deplorable conditions—the living death of solitary confinement and sensory deprivation—at Guantánamo and elsewhere were pioneered in supermax prisons like California's Pelican Bay and Florida's ADX Florence.

All of us who write about the human-rights violations that have accompanied the "war on terror" and the occupation of Iraq hope against hope that there is a foothold in our heritage for the principles we need to invoke. And maybe that hope is not wholly forlorn. But we have to read Dayan's book—and more studies like it—if we are to dispel the sort of wishful thinking that expects this set of practices simply to wither away when the present crisis is past. If Dayan is right, it will not wither away. It will retreat back into its natural habitat—the American way of disciplining a large and unwieldy prison population, a direct descendant of the American way of controlling a large population of slaves. It will retreat back into business as usual for our complacent and indifferent courts. For a while it won't be as visible as the torture memos or the Abu Ghraib photographs or the Jose Padilla videotape. But it will be there all the same—until the next time.

*Jeremy Waldron is a University Professor at* NYU *Law School. He is the author of "Torture and Positive Law: Jurisprudence for the White House," published in the* Columbia Law Review *in 2005.*

# THE STORY OF
# CRUEL AND UNUSUAL

# 1

DESCRIBING THE STANDARD TECH-
niques for interrogating Iraqis detained at
Abu Ghraib prison, Guy Womack, the lawyer defending Specialist Charles A. Graner
against charges of prisoner abuse, said that a
certain amount of violence does not "exceed
the norm": "Striking doesn't mean a lot.
Breaking a rib or bone—*that* would be excessive." Harvey Volzer, the lawyer for Specialist Megan M. Ambuhl, another of the
defendants, said that what his client had participated in was no worse than intimidation:
"I wouldn't term it abuse." Paul Bergrin, the

lawyer for a third defendant, Sergeant Javal S. Davis, said that his client's actions had caused no real harm. "He may have stepped on the hands, but there was no stomping, no broken bones." Secretary of Defense Donald Rumsfeld, answering questions at a Defense Department briefing, drew comparably subtle distinctions: "I'm not a lawyer. My impression is that what has been charged thus far is abuse, which I believe technically is different from torture."

The blurring of distinctions between intimidation and abuse, abuse and torture has a real legal history. It might seem at first that the rules for the treatment of Iraqi prisoners were founded on standards suited to war or emergencies, based on what the political theorist Carl Schmitt called the urgency of the "exception." They were meant to remain secret and to be exempt from traditional legal ideals and the courts associated with them. But the ominous discretionary powers used to justify this conduct are not exceptional; they are routine and entirely familiar to those who follow the everyday treatment of prisoners in the United States—in prison and in court. The now-famous "torture memos," written by lawyers in the White House and in the Departments of Defense and Justice, redefined the meaning of torture and extended the limits of permissible pain. Unprecedented as they appear, they rely upon the last 30 years of court decisions, which have gradually eviscerated the Eighth Amendment's prohibition of "cruel and unusual punishments."

But the problem of affixing meaning to these words is part of a much older story. Since the 18th century, "cruel" and "unusual" have been coupled in lasting intimacy in our legal language. And from the beginning the phrase has been vexed by ambiguity. Unlike due process, the business of cruel and unusual punishment does not have a history so much as a compulsive repetition; its jurisprudence cycles interminably between two poles: safeguarding rights and justifying their revocation.

The phrase "cruel and unusual punishments" first appeared in 1689 in the English Bill of Rights, drafted by Parliament at the accession of William and Mary. It seems to have been directed against punishments unauthorized by statute, beyond the jurisdiction of the sentencing court, or disproportionate to the offense committed. The American colonists incorporated the words into most of the original state constitutions. They became part of the American Bill of Rights in 1791 as the Eighth Amendment to the Constitution: "Excessive bail shall not be required, nor excessive fines imposed, nor cruel and unusual punishments inflicted."

The American draftsmen intended that the "cruel and unusual punishments" clause apply to "tortures" and other "barbarous" methods of punishment, such as pillorying, stretching on the rack, drawing and quartering, cutting off the hands or ears, branding on the hands or face, slitting the nostrils, or disemboweling. In other words, what mattered in the American context was unusual cruelty in the *method* of punishment, not the prohibition of excessive punishments.

If the methods of punishment used in the United States today—the death penalty, prolonged solitary confinement, extreme force, and psychological torture—seem barbaric by our standards and by those of the rest of the so-called civilized world, this can be traced to the colonial history of the legal stigmatization and deprivation of a group considered less than human.

The Supreme Court's most recent Eighth Amendment decisions, the ones underlying the torture memos, summon in new places and under new guises the genealogy of slavery and civil incapacitation.

# 2

THE ARGUMENT OF LEGITIMACY, SECU-
rity, and necessity has its most crucial, if
most concealed, history in legislation that
bolstered the institution of slavery. In *The
History, Civil and Commercial, of the British
Colonies in the West Indies* (1793), Bryan Ed-
wards described the logic of containment in
slave-holding countries: "The leading prin-
ciple on which the government is supported
is fear: or a sense of that absolute coercive
necessity which, leaving no choice of action,
supersedes all questions of right."

Given the lack of precedent in English law, the speed with which the institution of slavery took shape in the United States and the severity of the laws governing it are remarkable. The sources of these laws are much debated, but it seems clear that Roman civil law, slave codes in the Spanish and Portuguese possessions of the 15th and 16th century, the *Code Noir* of the French Antilles (1685), and the 18th-century laws of the British West Indies all contributed a language that at once offered protection and normalized abuse.

In her groundbreaking *The West Indian Slave Laws of the Eighteenth Century* (1970), the Jamaican historian Elsa V. Goveia describes how existing slave laws were codified to elicit obedience: while "the provisions safeguarding the slave as a person were either laxly enforced or neglected," she wrote, "the part of the law which provided for his control and submission continued in vigor." In the United States, statute and case law appeared to promise an alleviation of debasement: the master had no power over life and limb, and the letter of the law offered itself, at least nominally, to the spirit of Christianity. But such civil rituals did not so much alleviate the stigma of slavery as subtly move degradation into other modes.

Slave law defined the minimal needs of slaves in great detail. In 1861 the Alabama Supreme Court ruled in *Creswell's Executor v. Walker* that slaves, although dead to civil rights and responsibilities, must be provided with "a sufficiency of healthy food or necessary clothing … and the master cannot relieve himself of the legal obligation to supply the slave's necessary wants." Black codes and slave courts in the North American colonies, like those in the Caribbean, focused intensely on protecting the bodies of slaves even while allowing extreme mutilation. In many legal restrictions, the license to fall short of what might be considered humane lay in the unsaid—or in language that was deliberately unclear or hypothetical. This spurious generality, operating under cover of excessive legalism, is perhaps nowhere so pronounced as in the laws that made violence against slaves a necessary or ordinary part of slavery. According to John Haywood's *A Manual of the Laws of North Carolina* (1808), a person would not be judged "guilty of willfully and maliciously killing a slave" if the slave had died "under moderate correction." To style as "moderate" a "correction" that causes death is to assure that old abuses would continue, made legitimate by vague standards.

In *The Black Code of Georgia* (1732–
1899), assembled by W.E.B. Du Bois for
the Negro exhibit of the American section of
the Exposition Universelle in Paris in 1900,
the penal code amended and approved in
January 1851 lists prohibited acts of cruelty
against slaves: "unnecessary and excessive
whipping, beating, cutting or wounding or
… cruelly and unnecessarily biting or tearing with dogs … withholding proper food
and sustenance." When the use of whips,
cudgels, and dogs was not only possible but
to be expected, the effort to enshrine de-
scriptions of gratuitous and extreme cruelty
in law became only a guarantee of tyranny.
It allowed masters to hide behind the law
and ensured that their posture of care would
remain a humane fiction.

In *Turnipseed v. State* (1844), Chief Justice Henry W. Collier of the Alabama Su-

preme Court reversed a lower court's conviction of a man accused of beating his slave, Rachel, in a "cruel" manner. In overturning the indictment because of its "general terms," Collier spent a great deal of time interpreting the phrase "cruel and unusual punishment" as it applied to the treatment of slaves in the sixth chapter of the state penal code. "*Cruel*, as indicating the infliction of pain of either mind or body, is a word of most extensive application; yet every cruel punishment is not, perhaps, unusual; nor, perhaps, can it be assumed that every uncommon infliction is cruel." Using the phrase's ambiguity as an excuse for ignoring actual harm done, he denied that a crime had been committed. "We must hold the scales of justice in *equipoise*, and however odious the offence, we must admeasure right to every one according to law."

The abolitionist William Goodell in *The American Slave Code in Theory and Practice* (1853) denied that slave law was law at all: the Mississippi statute of 1822 barring the infliction of "cruel and unusual punishment … on any slave in this State" was only a hollow pretense: "And it is only an unusual punishment that is forbidden! The masters and overseers have only to repeat their excessive punishments so frequently that they become 'usual,' and the statute does not apply to them!"

Even after emancipation, to the extent that former slaves were allowed personalities before the law, they were regarded chiefly—almost solely—as potential criminals. During the second session of the 39th Congress (December 12, 1866–January 8, 1867) disagreements raged on the meaning of the exemption in the 13th Amendment to the

Constitution that abolished slavery "except as a punishment for crime whereof the party shall have been duly convicted." So those who were once slaves were now accused of petty crimes, convicted and jailed, and forced to labor in the convict-lease system, in which private companies leased prisoners from the state.

In *The Souls of Black Folk* (1903), Du Bois explained how formal emancipation had led to legal bondage: "When the Negroes were freed and the whole South was convinced of the impossibility of free Negro labor, the first and almost universal device was to use the courts as a means of reënslaving the blacks. It was not then a question of crime, but rather one of color." The ghost of slavery still haunts our legal language and holds the prison system in thrall.

# 3

PERPHAPS THE LEAST UNDERSTOOD PART
of the Constitution, the Eighth Amendment
is the only provision of the Bill of Rights
that explicitly relates to prisoners. It has no
landmark ruling, although it received its
broadest interpretation between the mid-
1960s and early 1980s, during the prisoners'
rights movement. As a limit on the state's
power to punish, the Eighth Amendment's
negative guarantee expands in importance
in the prison context.

Nearly two years before his appointment
to the Supreme Court, Justice Harry Black-

mun, then a member of the U.S. Court of Appeals for the Eighth Circuit, recognized the need to give substance to the Eighth Amendment. In *Jackson v. Bishop* (1968), he declared that the physical abuse of prisoners was cruel and unusual punishment under the Constitution. Arguing that debates over language represented a pretext for continued excess, he wrote, "We choose to draw no significant distinction between the word 'cruel' and the word 'unusual' in the Eighth Amendment."

Citing court decisions that had authorized whipping with a strap as punishment for not picking enough cotton or leaving cucumbers on the vine—whether limited to ten lashes, or carried out in the fields, or within 24 hours of any earlier whipping—Blackmun asked, "How does one, or any court, ascertain the point which would distinguish the permissible from that which is cruel and unusual?"

During this period the application of Eighth Amendment protections broadened. In *Laaman v. Helgemoe* (1977), the federal district court for New Hampshire held that conditions of confinement at New Hampshire State Prison in Concord constituted cruel and unusual punishment. The court's far-reaching relief order was the broadest application ever of the Eighth Amendment, not only acknowledging the limits it set on the punishment of "the physical body" but ruling that "its protections extend to the whole person as a human being." In a detailed opinion, the court found that confinement itself could violate the Constitution if it made prisoner "degeneration probable and reform unlikely." While recognizing that prisoners were "adequately warehoused," the

19

court denounced the inhumanity of "isolation cells" and the lack of educational programs and vocational training as "coerced stagnation."

The prisoners' rights era also temporarily ended the death penalty. Until the 1970s, the Supreme Court had protected it, ruling, for example, in *In re Kemmler* (1888) that although electrocution is "certainly unusual," it is not cruel. But in 1972, in *Furman v. Georgia*, the court declared capital punishment in its current form cruel and unusual, and therefore unconstitutional. In Justice William Brennan's words, the system of capital punishment was not only excessive and unnecessary but also irrational and arbitrary. Recalling Chief Justice Earl Warren's decision in *Trop v. Dulles* (1958), which had posited "the dignity of man" as the lynchpin of the Eighth Amendment, Brennan argued that the death penalty was "degrading to human dignity" and deprived the criminal of "human status." The court voted 5–4 to strike down every capital-punishment law in the United States. In a lengthy concurring opinion that included a survey of the English and American legal history of the term "cruel" and an assessment of the necessity and usefulness of such an extreme punishment in contemporary society, Thurgood Marshall wrote that "the use of the word 'unusual' in the English Bill of Rights of 1689 was inadvertent, and there is nothing in the history of the Eighth Amendment to give flesh to its intended meaning."

While Brennan and Marshall sought to make the Eighth Amendment a far-ranging prohibition against degrading and inhuman punishment, Chief Justice Burger in his dissent (which was joined by Blackmun, Powell, and William Rehnquist) set the tone for future interpretations. Burger wrote, "Of all our fundamental guarantees, the ban on 'cruel and unusual punishments' is one of the most difficult to translate into judicially manageable terms." This unmanageability, what Burger described as "the haze that surrounds this constitutional command," would later be used to redefine the limits of torture, and, at the extreme, define them away entirely.

Burger went on to argue that capital punishment is permissible as long as it is not barbarous. "It is not," he explained, "a punishment, such as burning at the stake, that everyone would ineffably find to be repugnant to all civilized standards." Within just two years, 28 state legislatures had retooled capital-sentencing laws to make them less "capricious," and the Supreme Court reinstated capital punishment in *Gregg v. Georgia* in 1976.

The shift away from expansive Eighth Amendment protections began in earnest in the 1980s with a series of cases challenging inadequacies in medical care, use of force, and conditions of confinement. In struggling to create a new framework for prison jurisprudence, the court sought to give specific meaning to words such as "cruelty," "pain," "injury," and "punishment." But in the end, this wave of legal decisions weakened existing standards and obscured the harm and indignity suffered by prisoners by focusing attention on the motivations of prison officials.

Writing for the majority in *Rhodes v. Chapman* (1981), Justice Powell found no constitutional mandate for "comfortable prisons" and argued that conditions such

23

as prison overcrowding do not fall within the scope of "serious deprivations of basic human needs" by contemporary standards. He argued that, in relation to the horrific conditions in two Arkansas prisons deemed unconstitutional in *Hutto v. Finney* (1978), the double celling of inmates in the present case (among other discomforts) was not serious enough to violate the constitutional standard: "To the extent that such conditions are restrictive, and even harsh, they are part of the penalty that criminal offenders pay for their offenses against society." Therefore, short of causing unnecessary and wanton pain, "deprivations … simply are not punishments." He did not specify the degree of severity that would violate the Eighth Amendment, but, significantly, he suggested a policy of deference to the penal philosophy of prison officials.

24

However, it was only when William Hubbs Rehnquist became chief justice in 1986 that the court fully revealed its talent for defining away the substance of the Eighth Amendment. The Rehnquist court, in turning fully to the "subjective" expertise of prison administrators and offering "deference" to their special knowledge, raised the threshold beyond which any particular harm is legally relevant; conditions in the prison environment could no longer constitute punishment. The winnowing away of the substance of incarceration—what actually happens to the inmate—in favor of a vague system of rules and labels has allowed increasingly abnormal circumstances to be normalized. In this juridical calculation, what is harsh, brutal, or excessive turns into what is constitutional, customary, or just bearable.

Moreover, this language constructs a legal person who stands in a negative relation to law, who has no rights, and whose fundamental status thus remains distinct from all others.

# 4

THE SUBJECTIVE REQUIREMENT THAT
marked the Rehnquist Court's Eighth
Amendment decisions depended on an
earlier case. In *Louisiana ex rel. Francis v.
Resweber* (1947), Willie Francis, a "colored
citizen," was sentenced to death by a Louisiana court. The attempted electrocution
failed due to mechanical difficulties, and
Francis petitioned the Supreme Court, arguing that a second attempt to execute him
would be unconstitutionally cruel. Justice
Stanley Reed, writing for the majority, ruled
against Francis. Even though Francis had al-

ready suffered the effects of an electrical current, that did not "make his subsequent execution any more cruel in the constitutional sense than any other execution. The cruelty against which the Constitution protects a convicted man is cruelty inherent in the method of punishment, not the necessary suffering involved in any method employed to extinguish life humanely." The dissenting justices understood Francis's experience to be akin to "torture culminating in death," and asked, "How many deliberate and intentional reapplications of electric current does it take to produce a cruel, unusual and unconstitutional punishment?"

While granting that the Eighth Amendment prohibited "the wanton infliction of pain" and conceding that Francis would now be forced again to undergo the mental anguish of preparing for death, Reed's majority opinion gave legal weight to the state's *intent*: "There is no purpose to inflict unnecessary pain, nor any unnecessary pain involved in the proposed execution. The situation of the unfortunate victim of this accident is just as though he had suffered the identical amount of mental anguish and physical pain in any other occurrence, such as, for example, a fire in the cell block."

The intent requirement of *Louisiana ex rel. Francis v. Resweber* would become the controlling precedent for later cases that analyzed how the "cruel and unusual punishments" standard applied to the conditions of a prisoner's confinement. In *Duckworth v. Franzen* (1985), a year before Rehnquist's confirmation, Judge Richard Posner, writing for the U.S. Court of Appeals for the Seventh Circuit, concluded that shackled prisoners who were injured during transport when their bus caught fire had not been subjected to cruel and unusual punishment. The intent requirement had not been met, since the officers had not intended "maliciously" to cause harm: "Negligence, perhaps; gross negligence … perhaps; but not cruel and unusual punishment." What happened was nothing more than "if the guard accidentally stepped on the prisoner's toe and broke it."

Invoking Samuel Johnson's *A Dictionary of the English Language*, Posner defined "punishment" as "Any infliction or pain imposed in vengeance of a crime." In other words, punishment is decreed by the sentencing judge and has nothing to do with what happens afterward, whether deprivations within or accidents outside a prison. Only "malicious intent," not what Justice Felix Frankfurter in his concurrence to *Loui-*

*siana ex rel. Francis v. Resweber* had called "an innocent misadventure," could make unconstitutional what prisoners suffered after incarceration, no matter how harmful to their minds and bodies.

The majority opinion in *Gregg v. Georgia*, which overturned *Furman v. Georgia* and reinstated capital punishment, coined the phrase "unnecessary and wanton infliction of pain." But it was the Rehnquist court, and especially Justice Antonin Scalia's precedent-setting opinion in *Wilson v. Seiter* (1991), that gave the intent requirement and the word "wantonness" their fiercest play. It would prove to be the most crucial Eighth Amendment prison case in a decade.

Pearly Wilson, an inmate at the Hocking Correctional Facility in Ohio, brought a *pro se* lawsuit alleging that conditions in the prison, including overcrowding, excessive noise, inadequate heating and ventilation, unsanitary dining facilities, and lack of protection from communicable diseases, violated the Eighth Amendment. Writing for the five-member majority (Rehnquist, O'Connor, Kennedy, Souter, and himself), Scalia relied on Posner's definition of punishment in *Duckworth v. Franzen*—"a deliberate act intended to chastise or deter"—and on a "subjective" standard of intent derived from another case, *Estelle v. Gamble* (1976), which deemed "deliberate indifference to serious medical needs" unconstitutional, to set an impossibly high bar for Eighth Amendment violations.

*Estelle* had presented two alternatives for establishing Eighth Amendment violations: either they are incompatible with (quoting *Trop v. Dulles*) "the evolving standards of decency that mark the progress of a maturing society" or they (quoting *Gregg v. Georgia*) "involve the unnecessary and wanton infliction of pain." *Wilson* made no allowance for such a choice. It recognized as prohibited only "obduracy and wantonness, not inadvertence or error in good faith," language drawn from the earlier case of *Whitley v. Alpers* (1986). Whether the context is a prison disturbance, medical care, or conditions of confinement, the preoccupation here is with the knowledge, deliberation, or intent of those in control. If not a specific part of the prisoner's sentence, then, deprivations are not really punishment unless they are imposed by officers with "a sufficiently culpable state of mind." In other words, no matter how much actual suffering is experienced by a prisoner, it cannot be deemed unconstitutional unless the intent requirement is met.

Elizabeth Alexander, of the ACLU National Prison Project, argued for the plaintiffs that no inquiry into state of mind should mitigate unconstitutional conditions, which are often the result of accumulated actions over time. She explained that the "government has an affirmative duty to supply the basic necessities of life to those whom it has deprived of the ability to supply those necessities on their own." Her complaint was less with the two-pronged objective and subjective test than with the idea that the judging of objective conditions could be replaced entirely with suppositions about the subjective thoughts of prison officials and deference to their explanations. "The point of injunctive relief is to end the suffering, not to fix the blame," Alexander said.

But the *Wilson* majority was not listening. It ruled that general prison conditions cannot cumulatively reach the level of cruel and unusual punishment unless they "have a mutually enforcing effect that produces the deprivation of a single, identifiable human need such as food, warmth, or exercise—for example, a low cell temperature at night combined with a failure to issue blankets." By focusing on discrete "necessities," the court ignored the moral and emotional degeneration that had been so decried in lower federal court cases in the 1970s. In disregarding anything "so amorphous as 'overall conditions,'" Scalia dismantled the "totality of circumstances" test established in *Laaman v. Helgemoe,* which had condemned "the cold storage of human beings" and "enforced idleness" as nothing less than a "numbing violence against the human spirit."

Scalia's opinion in *Wilson* led to the reproduction of conditions that disfigure personhood and incapacitate prisoners—those amorphous abuses that have nothing to do with lighting, food, clothing, shelter, or medical care. Using reasoning reminiscent of 19th-century slave law, the court in effect established that a broad and systematic deprivation that causes psychological harm—for example, indefinite detention in administrative segregation—is not unconstitutional as long as it serves a legitimate correctional purpose. But what are legitimate correctional purposes when those incarcerated are arbitrarily assumed to be dangerous, unfit, and subhuman?

A critical change has occurred within the domain of corrections. Though many of those incarcerated in state prisons in the United States are not violent offenders, they are exposed to the most public degradation—warehoused indefinitely, put to work on chain gangs, attacked by dogs, shackled to walls, shocked with tasers. Prisoners' crimes no longer explain their treatment; rather, society is inventing the criminal, creating a new class of the condemned.

# 5

THROUGH OFTEN INGENIOUS LEGAL maneuvers, the Supreme Court has paved the way for cruelty in prison life that passes for necessary or commonplace. Deprivation or injury matters only when "sufficiently serious," when involving "more than ordinary lack of due care," or inflicting "substantial pain." Conditions such as indefinite solitary confinement are thus unconstitutional only if they result from malicious intent or pose a "substantial risk of serious harm."

In *Hudson v. McMillian* (1992), Keith Hudson, an inmate at the state penitentiary in Angola, Louisiana, sued three corrections officers for punching him in the eyes, mouth, chest, and stomach. The bruises were minor, but there was swelling of Hudson's face, mouth, and lip; the officers also cracked his dental plate and loosened his teeth. The supervisor on duty watched the beating and advised his officers, "Don't have too much fun." Justice Sandra Day O'Connor wrote for the 7–2 majority that, given the officers' malicious and sadistic intent, the use of excessive physical force could constitute cruel and unusual punishment even if no "serious injury" resulted.

Even though the majority opinion rejected the federal appeals court's assertion of a "significant injury" requirement (leaving permanent marks or requiring medical attention), the victory for prisoners was qualified. The malice standard O'Connor applied, which was derived from *Whitley v. Albers*, had in that case been limited to the use of force in a prison riot. By extending the application of this exacting standard—rather than the "unnecessary and wanton infliction of pain" standard—to *all* cases involving allegations of excessive physical force, *Hudson* increased the burden of proof to one that would be all but impossible for plaintiffs to meet.

Aware of what the court left unsaid and trying to turn attention back to actual harm done, Justice Blackmun in his concurring opinion stressed that mental as well as physical harm mattered: "As the Court makes clear, the Eighth Amendment prohibits the unnecessary and wanton infliction of 'pain,' rather than 'injury.' … 'Pain' in its ordinary meaning surely includes a notion of psychological harm."

Justice Clarence Thomas, joined by Scalia, wrote in his dissent that the judgment had not only ignored the "significant injury" requirement but had wrenched the Eighth Amendment and the word "punishment" itself "from its historical moorings." If we accept the rack, the thumbscrew, the wheel, and other ingenious forms of mutilation as the context for the constitutional guarantee, then a mere beating, an "entirely physical" injury might well fail to be "sufficiently serious." Indeed, Thomas argued that the meaning of "punishment" in Eighth Amendment cases should be narrowed to "penalties meted out by statutes or sentencing judges," not a "broad range of prison deprivations." He wrote, "A use of force that causes only insignificant harm to a prisoner may be immoral, it may be tortious, it may be criminal, and it may even be remediable under other provisions of the Federal Constitution, but it is not 'cruel and unusual punishment.'"

Cruelty takes many forms other than the corporeal, as even Thomas recognized in *Hudson*, but what is striking about contemporary Eighth Amendment cases, whether dealing with execution or confinement, is the affirmation of the corporal-punishment paradigm, attending only to the body and not to the mind (ignoring, for example, psychological pain and fear) or to the prisoner's place in society—concerns that were once deemed vital to human dignity and worth.

What are the minimal conditions of existence deemed tolerable for prisoners? In *Madrid v. Gomez* (1995)—a class-action suit against the California Department of Corrections heard by the U.S. District Court for the Northern District of California—prisoners incarcerated at Pelican Bay State Prison challenged the constitutionality of a broad range of conditions and practices. Chief Judge Thelton Henderson condemned the habit of caging inmates naked outdoors in freezing temperatures like "animals in a zoo"; the unnecessary and sometimes lethal force used in forcibly removing an inmate from his cell; and the scalding of a mentally disabled black inmate, burned so badly that "from just below the buttocks down, his skin had peeled off." An officer had said mockingly, "Looks like we're going to have a white boy before this is through."

Finding in the plaintiffs' favor, Henderson wrote that "defendants have unmistakably crossed the constitutional line with respect to some of the claims raised by this action," citing failure to provide adequate medical and mental-health care and encouragement of systematic and excessive force. He reserved his greatest condemnation for conditions in the "security housing unit," a separate, self-contained, super-maximum-security complex. Yet indefinite solitary confinement in the SHU did not for all inmates cross over into the realm of "psychological torture." Although Henderson acknowledged that conditions in the SHU might cause "psychological trauma," such conditions remain within the limits of the permissible. They do not per se violate "exacting Eighth Amendment standards."

Other contemporary decisions have retooled slavery for the 21st century. Under cover of "legitimacy" and "reasonableness," using terms like "decency" and "basic human needs," the courts have sustained a brutalization that might not leave physical

45

marks but that recreates the civil, legal, and political incapacitation of slavery. What is the status of inmates in our prisons? Thanks to the Rehnquist court, they are effectively dead in law, a penalty that is felt perhaps nowhere so powerfully as in the question of access to the courts, the most fundamental of rights.

In *Lewis v. Casey* (1996), the Supreme Court overturned the decisions of a district court and a court of appeals, which had ruled inadequate the law libraries and legal-assistance programs in the Arizona state prison system. Justice Antonin Scalia, delivering the majority opinion, denied the rights or needs of prisoners to discover grievances and to litigate effectively once in court—to "transform themselves," as he put it, "into litigating engines." By the time the majority—which ranged from five to eight justices depending on the issue being considered—decided the case, plans were already in place to gut existing libraries in the Arizona prison system and to substitute forms, pencils, and bilingual paralegals for law libraries, legal assistants, and the right to conduct research or ask the state for assistance.

In his dissent, Justice Stevens recognized the unprecedented nature of a 20th-century ruling that could secure legal incapacity. He summoned the ghost of a 19th-century case, *Ruffin v. Commonwealth* (1871), in which justices were called on to consider the applicability of the Virginia constitution's bill of rights to the case of Woody Ruffin, a convict charged with the murder of a fellow prisoner on a chain gang in Bath, Virginia. Justice Joseph Christian ruled, "The bill of rights is a declaration of general principles to govern a society of freemen, and not of convicted felons and men civilly dead. Such men have some rights it is true, such as the law in its benignity accords them, but not the rights of freemen. They are the slaves of the State undergoing punishment for heinous crimes committed against the laws of the land." Stevens wrote in *Lewis*, "While at least one 19th-century court characterized the prison inmate as a mere 'slave of the State,' … in recent decades this Court has repeatedly held that the convicted felon's loss of liberty is not total … The 'well-established' right of access to the courts … is one of these aspects of liberty that States must affirmatively protect."

As the Rehnquist court delivered increasingly harsh decisions in cases concerning the punishment, transfer, confinement, and segregation of prisoners, dissenting justices—Justices Marshall, Brennan, and Stevens—recalled *Ruffin* to condemn the present-day treatment of prisoners as dead in law. They were naming the precedent for the state-sanctioned bondage the court was affirming.

# 6

In Furman v. Georgia, Justice Brennan had argued that there could be cruelty worse than bodily pain or mutilation. It was not just "the presence of pain" that was significant in relation to the Eighth Amendment, he argued, but the treatment of "members of the human race as *nonhumans*, as objects to be toyed with and discarded." Slave codes in the South had required only that slaves receive clothing, food, and lodging "sufficient to their basic needs." Like the slave whose brute body had yet to be protected against unnecessary mutilation or torture, the criminal is reduced in present-day law to nothing but the physical person.

The Prison Litigation Reform Act (tacked onto a spending bill by Congress), which President Bill Clinton signed into law on April 26, 1996, dramatically curtailed the ability of prisoners to litigate. Designed to limit what was said to be a massive increase in "frivolous" inmate litigation, the act permits injunctive relief related to prison conditions but erects substantial hurdles that must be negotiated before such relief can be given. Plaintiffs must prove that every member of their group or proposed class has suffered physical injury before claiming mental or emotional injury. They must prove that their request for relief is narrowly focused, extends no further than necessary to correct the injury, and is the least intrusive means to correct or prevent the harm. As an inmate wrote to me, "Only prisoners are excluded from relief or damages stemming from mental pain or suffering (as if such pains are rightfully reserved for us alone)."

This realm of constitutional minimums—situated between mere need and bare survival—set the stage for Guantánamo Bay and Abu Ghraib. I recall the words of Marine Brigadier General Michael R. Lehnert at Guantánamo Bay in 2002: "There is no torture, no whips, no bright lights, no drugging. We are a nation of laws."

But what kind of laws? Laws that permit indefinite solitary confinement in state-of-the-art units, with cell doors, unit doors, and shower doors operated remotely from a control center and physical contact limited to touching through a security door by a correctional officer while being placed in restraints. Inmates have described life in the massive, windowless super-maximum prison as akin to "living in a tomb," "circling in space," or "being freeze-dried."

Nowhere does the power of penal law to revoke civil rights and legal capacities become as evident as in the case of solitary confinement. Over the past two and a half decades, an intimate dialogue between courts and prison administrators has normalized what was once the most severe deprivation. The subject is couched in euphemisms: first "disciplinary segregation," and later "administrative segregation" (nominally based on security classification rather than wrongdoing). Since prison officials claim that these units are non-punitive, they are difficult to fight under either the Eighth or the Fourteenth Amendment.

Since the 1980s, the United Nations Commission on Human Rights, the United

Nations Committee Against Torture, the Red Cross, human-rights organizations such as Amnesty International and Human Rights Watch, and civil-rights organizations such as the ACLU and the Center for Constitutional Rights, have criticized the darkly authoritarian and abusive conditions of prisons in the United States, focusing on super-maximum imprisonment, where inmates deemed incorrigible are locked down for 23 to 24 hours a day, their food delivered through a slot in the steel door of their 80-square-foot cell.

These supermaxes (also known as "special treatment," "special management," "special housing," or "security housing" units) justify their existence through the typology of a particular kind of prisoner, who has attained the status of "the worst of the worst." Though assumed to be a threat to prison security, these inmates have often committed no overt act or exhibited any violent behavior behind bars. Segregation decisions are based upon status—alleged gang affiliation, for example—not evidence of any infraction of prison rules. In other words, judgments of "criminal will" are made regardless of criminal action; notions about innate character or general disposition largely replace misconduct. Prisoners are classified into "security-threat groups" (meaning gangs), "special-needs groups" (meaning the psychologically disabled), or "assaultive" (meaning never divulged). Once branded, these inmates are held under "close" or "secure" management.

These extreme strategies have become especially significant as the Washington authorities export their prisons, prison administrators, and even correctional officers to the Middle East, Haiti, and elsewhere. The new global logic of punishment promises democracy while requiring no judge and jury; and it ensures the broader establishment of lucrative super-maximum security units. Once stigmatized categories are created, whether they are labeled "security-threat groups" or "illegal enemy combatants," torture can be administered readily by those in power.

# 7

THE REHNQUIST COURT'S EIGHTH
Amendment cases prepared the ground for
the verbal quibbles, fastidious distinctions,
and parsing of definitions that characterize
the memoranda prepared for the "war on
terror." The legal nullification of personhood that began with slavery has been per-
fected through the logic of the courtroom
and adjusted to apply to prisoners. This reasoning—so long ignored, except by some
corrections officials—was carefully studied
by the White House lawyers charged with
reviewing the legal limits of torture.

The torture memos of August 1, 2002, (sent by Assistant Attorney General Jay S. Bybee to the White House counsel, Alberto Gonzales) and March 6, 2003, (drafted by a Defense Department working group) reveal the same obsessive concern with intent and the same indifference to objective conditions as the prison cases discussed earlier. Whether an interrogator has maimed, blinded, or killed a detainee does not matter unless the interrogator *intended* to maim, blind, or kill. A subsection of the March 6, 2003, memorandum entitled "Specifically Intended" explains that violation of the federal "torture statute" (18 U.S.C. 2340) "requires that severe pain and suffering must be inflicted with specific intent," meaning that the defendant "must have expressly intended to achieve the forbidden act." He even gets another loophole: his intent can be nullified if he had "a good faith belief" that whatever he did would not result in mutilation or death. The results—a mutilated, blind, or dead body—get defined away by the vain search for intent, and the defendant who committed the act is (if the jury cooperates) vindicated.

In a memorandum to the president on January 25, 2002, Gonzales argued that the Geneva Convention rules governing the treatment and interrogation of prisoners had been rendered "obsolete" and "quaint." What, then, were the relevant restrictions that the degradations and abuses of prisoners in Iraq, Afghanistan, and Guantánamo were crafted to circumvent? It was that other set of rules, the U.S. laws and court rulings governing prisoners and punishment.

The third section of the March 6, 2003, memorandum, titled "Domestic Law," while adopting much of the legal language and logic of the August 1, 2002, memo, differs in its critical focus on prison law. The March 6 memo makes explicit use of recent Eighth Amendment decisions that were absent from the earlier memo, presenting a chilling recapitulation of the cases discussed here. The memo cites *Ingraham v. Wright* (1977), which held that the Eighth Amendment prohibition of cruel and unusual punishments was "designed to protect those convicted of crimes." Since detainees are not charged with, let alone convicted of, any crimes, it argues, "assuming a detainee could establish standing to challenge his treatment, the claim would not lie under the 8th Amendment."

In a fractured, powerfully condensed subsection (just four pages), the memo analyzes the constitutional standards of the

Eighth Amendment, the determination of criminal intent and significant injury. The precise legal justification for skirting the character of punishment is distilled from Supreme Court decisions. The memo quotes *Wilson v. Seiter*: all claims about unacceptable prison conditions must show "deliberate indifference" to the conditions of prisoners. And it reiterates the *Wilson* majority's refusal to recognize anything "so amorphous as 'overall conditions'" of confinement, focusing instead on the actual, physical, "specific deprivation of a single human need."

The quibbling over such terms as "severe," "significant," "extreme," and "serious" neutralizes the obvious and trivializes abuse. In the March 6, 2003, memorandum, for example, the legal analysis relies particularly on the definition of the term "severe" in the torture statute in federal criminal law.

Torture is defined as any "act committed by a person acting under the color of law specifically intended to inflict severe physical or mental pain." But the Pentagon lawyers, under the pretense of following the Supreme Court's dictum to "construe a statutory term in accordance with its ordinary or natural meaning," turn to their dictionaries.

This a crucial gesture repeated throughout the memo. The pile-up of references—to *Webster's New International Dictionary*, *The American Heritage Dictionary of the English Language*, and *The Oxford English Dictionary*—leads from the discussion of "severe" to a list of what constitutes "prolonged mental harm," which ushers in further equivocation about the meaning of "prolonged," which is interpreted as "lasting, though not necessarily permanent damage." Once schooled in rituals of redefinition, the lawyers turn again to their dictionaries to apply these terms to the new situation (to "terrorists" rather than "criminals"). They parse words to a degree that goes far beyond the practice of the courts in order to derive legal standards of interrogation in this "war without end."

The March 6 memorandum also discusses why the United States imposed reservations to the United Nations Convention Against Torture and Other Cruel, Inhuman, or Degrading Treatment or Punishment, or UNCAT (which first came into force on June 26, 1987, and which the United States ratified on October 21, 1994). The convention prohibits torture "only as defined in the U.S. Understanding" and "other acts of cruel, inhuman or degrading treatment or punishment" (discussed in Article 16) only to the extent that they are already prohibited by the U.S. Constitution. The writers of the

65

memorandum justified their narrowing of the convention's protections by arguing that "the meaning of the term 'degrading treatment' was vague and ambiguous."

Amnesty International's "A Briefing for the UN Committee Against Torture" (May 2000), not only rebuked the United States for its treatment of prisoners, of whom over 60 percent are African-Americans or other racial minorities, but also warned that the United States' reservation to Article 16 "can apply to any US laws or practices which may breach international standards for humane treatment but are allowed under the US Constitution, for example, prolonged isolation or the use of electro-shock weapons."

In refusing to be bound by international standards of humane treatment, the United States finds another way to close its eyes to deleterious prison conditions while deferring to prison administrators. These conditions contravene not only UNCAT but the International Covenant on Civil and Political Rights (1966) and the Geneva Convention Relative to the Treatment of Prisoners of War (1949).

But nowhere do the unfortunate results of the United States' definitional sleight-of-hand become so obvious as in Senator John McCain's torture ban, Amendment No. 1977, approved by Congress as part of its $453.5 billion 2006 defense budget on December 22, 2005, and incorporated as the Detainee Treatment Act of 2005. Although the McCain amendment begins with a section called "Prohibition on Cruel, Inhuman, or Degrading Treatment or Punishment of Persons Under Custody or Control of the United States Government" and uses wording from the Army Field Manual that follows the Geneva Convention's protections of prisoners of war, its next section, "Uniform Standards for the Interrogation of Persons under the Detention of the Department of Defense," adopts the language of the U.S. reservations to UNCAT, forbidding only the treatment "prohibited by the Fifth, Eighth, and Fourteenth Amendments to the Constitution of the United States."

This narrow definition only distances us more from international humanitarian treaties, perpetuating the very treatment the act claims to condemn. Further, to placate the White House, which lobbied members of Congress to insert loopholes into the proposed prohibition, McCain added a legal defense for accused CIA and military interrogators that mimed the exculpatory logic of the torture memos. Threatening death and inflicting pain would be actionable only when the interrogator intended to harm. Torturous acts could be defended if the perpetrator, assumed to be "a person of ordinary sense and understanding," acted in good faith—in other words, if the government employee "did not know that the practices were unlawful."

The Detainee Treatment Act also includes the Graham-Levin Amendment, which strips federal courts of jurisdiction over detainees at Guantánamo, denying them the right to challenge their detention. Besides curbing the legal procedures promised under *Rasul v. Bush* (2004), this amendment also allows review boards to consider evidence gleaned as a result of torture or cruel and inhuman treatment.

Wisely, the Supreme Court on June 29, 2006, in *Hamdan v. Rumsfeld*, ruled 5–3 that the military commissions used to try detainees are unconstitutional and contravene international law. Writing for the majority, Justice Stevens indicated that at the very least, Common Article 3 of the Geneva Conventions protects those the Bush administration has called "illegal enemy combatants," a label that has no legal basis in U.S. or international law. He referred to Article 3's ban on "'the passing of sentences and the carrying out of executions without … affording all the judicial guarantees which are recognized as indispensable by civilized peoples," as well as its prohibition against "outrages upon personal dignity, in particular humiliating and degrading treatment," whether in the contexts of detention or interrogation procedures.

The White House has continued to insist on the "ambiguity" of Article 3. As in the torture memos, definition after definition guts the substance of "cruel, inhuman or degrading," and the more specific the analysis of what is obviously torture, the more arbitrary the definition becomes. The Defense Department promised a major policy reversal after the *Hamdan* decision, but it is quite likely that the White House lawyers will limit Article 3's prohibitions to corporeal and visible outrages, ignoring what they describe as "less extreme" or "alternative" forms of mistreatment. In light of past interpretations of "moderate abuse" by the Bush administration and actual practices in U.S. prisons at home and abroad, treatments such as sensory deprivation, behavior adjustment, and radical isolation will doubtless be ruled acceptable.

# 8

AGAINST THIS BACKDROP THE UNITED
Nations Commission on Human Rights
issued a devastating report on February 15,
2006, criticizing the Bush administration
for using domestic standards to define away
its human-rights obligations under international law. Calling for the immediate re-
lease of the detainees held at Guantánamo,
the five authors (experts appointed by the
commission) were especially concerned that
the United States was deliberately position-
ing itself to employ "certain interrogation
techniques that would not be permitted un-

der the internationally accepted definition of torture." In their report, the experts explained the Unites States' legal obligations, condemning arbitrary and ineffective confinement, "prolonged isolation," "cultural and religious harassment," "sensory deprivation," "intimidation," "excessive force," and "prolonged detention in Maximum Security Units."

The experts also noted that there had been over 350 acts of self-harm at Guantánamo in 2003 alone—individual and mass suicide attempts as well as prolonged hunger strikes. The largest hunger strike, in which 131 detainees participated, ended in 2006 with force-feeding through nose tubes, a process involving excruciating pain, bleeding, and vomiting. Talking to a group of reporters about the chair to which detainees were strapped during the insertion of the feeding tubes, General John Craddock, the head of the United States Southern Command, said, "It's not like 'The Chair.' It's a chair. It's pretty comfortable; it's not abusive." He explained how his soldiers gave detainees a choice of colors for feeding tubes—yellow, clear, and beige—adding, "They like the yellow."

As a party to UNCAT, the United States is required to present a report to the UN Committee Against Torture every four years describing its compliance with the convention. On May 6, 2005, the United States filed its second periodic report. A year later, on May 5 and May 8, 2006, in Geneva, the U.S. delegation, in its first appearance before the committee in six years, answered questions on topics that included Washington's interpretation of the absolute ban on global torture, its interrogation methods in prisons including Abu Ghraib and Guantánamo, the domestic misuse of shackles and other restraints, the chaining of detainees together in gangs or individually to hitching posts, and, most importantly, the use of solitary confinement. The committee also asked how "prolonged and indefinite detention with or without charges" and the possibility of consequent mental deterioration was "compatible with the obligation of the State party under article 16."

While apologizing for the "mistreatment" of Iraqi detainees, John B. Bellinger III, the U.S. State Department's legal adviser, claimed that there have been "relatively few actual cases of abuse and wrongdoing" by U.S. personnel abroad.

Meanwhile, the ACLU presented the committee with a petition signed by 51,000 Americans asserting that the government was responsible for "torture, government kidnapping, and indefinite detention." The petition demanded that the U.S. delegation respond directly to the universal prohibition against torture.

The ACLU also presented the committee with its detailed report *Enduring Abuse: Torture and Cruel Treatment by the United States at Home and Abroad* (April 2006), asserting a link between torture and abuse at Guantánamo, Afghanistan's Bagram Air Base, Abu Ghraib, and the CIA's "black sites"—secret detention centers in Eastern Europe and elsewhere—and the barbarous practices in the prisons and jails of the United States. The report's documentation of conditions of confinement in the United States and the lack of redress for inmates who seek damages for mental or emotional injury is necessary background for any consideration of the treatment of detainees in U.S. custody throughout the world.

On May 19, 2006, the UN Committee Against Torture formally released its findings. Though it "welcomed" the U.S. statement "that all officials, from all Government agencies, including its contractors, were prohibited from engaging in cruel, inhuman or degrading treatment or punishment," it refuted a number of assertions made by the United States.

At a press conference that day, Bellinger complained that the committee's report exhibited "numerous errors of fact, just simply things that they've got wrong about what the U.S. law or practice is." The exhaustive presentation of the United States included more than 200 pages of written answers to the committee's questions. The committee had questioned conditions in several supermaximum security units, as well as the shackling of female prisoners during child-birth and other uses "of shackles or other restraints in both federal and state prisons." Speaking for the U.S. delegation—a team of more than two dozen senior officials—Bell-inger quoted the language of U.S. Supreme Court decisions: "It should be noted that the use of shackles on prisoners is not per se unconstitutional," since that charge only ap-plies to measures that are "'unnecessary and wanton inflictions of pain,' that is, 'totally without penological justification.'"

Responding to a question from the com-mittee about solitary confinement and its compatibility with Article 16, Bellinger re-jected the label "solitary confinement" in favor of "disciplinary segregation" and "ad-ministrative segregation." The latter—and here Bellinger demonstrated his effective manipulation of correctional law—is "non-punitive in nature." He explained, "It is used to achieve separation from the general population when the inmate's presence in that population poses a 'serious threat to life, property, self, staff or other inmates, or to the security or orderly running' of the facility." He concluded, "The United States takes exception to the assumption contained in the question that prolonged isolation and indefinite detention *per se* constitute cruel, inhuman, or degrading treatment or punishment."

Both in his oral and written responses to the committee, Bellinger refused to explain the continued U.S. reservation to Article 16, or to answer the following request: "In practical terms," the committee asked in Question 43 of its "List of issues to be examined," if the U.S. continues to limit "the meaning of cruel, inhuman or degrading treatment or punishment to the treatment or punishment prohibited by the Fifth, Eighth and Fourteenth Amendments to the Constitution ... what kinds of treatment or punishment are prohibited, and admissible, by the amendments but not by the Convention?" Hoping to avoid any prevarication by the United States, the committee concluded by asking for "concrete examples" of allowable punishment.

Bellinger, using the repetitiveness and doubletalk that this administration has made its hallmark, complained that the language of Article 16—"cruel, inhuman or degrading treatment"—was so ambiguous that it was "difficult to state with certainty and precision what treatment or punishment, in the absence of a clarifying reservation, would be prohibited by Article 16, but permitted by the reservation. It is this very uncertainty that prompted the reservation in the first place." Then he mused about whether tasers, stun guns, or restraint chairs would be "covered by Article 16 of the Convention absent the United States reservation." Since the committee in Question 43 pressed him to explain the "compatibility" of the use of these devices with Article 16, Bellinger considered U.S. law regarding excessive force in prisons. Without equivocation, he justified atrocity as long as it was done right: "Courts have routinely upheld the lawfulness and constitutionality of such practices when employed correctly."

Almost two years earlier, and less than a week before the hearings that would result in the confirmation of Alberto Gonzales as attorney general of the United States, a memo supposedly repudiating and replacing the previous memos was posted unannounced on the Justice Department's Web site. The 17-page memorandum, "for James B. Comey, Deputy Attorney General," was dated December 30, 2004, and was written by Daniel Levin, the head of the Justice Department's office of legal counsel.

The Levin memorandum began with a proclamation that the United States opposes torture. Any discussion of domestic prison cases or determination of mental culpability or significant injury has been omitted. What remains is the over-definition that defines nothing at all: adding the word "extreme" to clarify the meaning of the word "severe" in contexts that aim to distinguish "torture" from "other acts of cruel, inhuman or degrading treatment." Under "The meaning of 'severe,'" repeating the dictionary definitions of the previous memos and making equivocal distinctions between gradations of pain, the memo regards torture, following UNCAT, as an "extreme form of 'cruel, inhuman or degrading treatment.'" What follows is a list of some of the kinds of "extreme conduct" that, according to the Levin memorandum, fall "within the statutory definition" of torture: "severe beatings to the genitals, head, and other parts of the body with metal pipes, brass knuckles, batons, a baseball bat ... removal of teeth with pliers ... cutting off ... fingers, pulling out ... fingernails." But these excesses lie at the outer limits of the barbarous. Any lesser atrocity is permitted.

Note that although the administration claimed that the previous torture memos had been superseded by the Levin memo, Bellinger's answer to Question 43 resurrects not only the "good faith" argument but some of the very Eighth Amendment cases of the March 6, 2003, memo that had made futile the invocation of the cruel and unusual punishments clause. Bellinger provides a carefully articulated legal rationale for what he calls "less-lethal weapons," since the incapacitation of "a targeted individual" is not *intended* to cause death. Referring to *Hudson v. McMillian* (and quoting *Whitley v. Albers*), Bellinger explains that the death of "a post-sentencing inmate" is unconstitutional only "if the force was inflicted 'maliciously and sadistically to cause harm,' rather than in a 'good faith effort to maintain or restore discipline.'"

# 9

THOMAS COBB, IN HIS INQUIRY INTO *the Law of Negro Slavery in the United States of America* (1858), explained how the subordination of the slave could be accommodated in law. Although killing a slave was murder, there were always loopholes. Degrees of injury were allowed. The category of prohibited violence was increasingly narrowed, and the law failed to redress harm if words could define it away.

The twisted logic of slavery had always done something pernicious to the language of punishment. Faced with the need to recognize the slave both as a person in law and as a unique species of property, the framers of the U.S. Constitution chose to adopt the language of the English Bill of Rights when they prohibited cruel and unusual punishments. They could have used the words of the Reverend Nathaniel Ward's *Body of Liberties,* adopted by the Massachusetts General Court in 1641. Compared with contemporary English law, it was ahead of its time, especially in its latitude with regard to criminal penalties. Clause 46 read, "For bodily punishments we allow amongst us none that are inhumane, barbarous, or cruel."

Slavery was introduced into the American colony of Virginia in 1619, and slaves became objects of legislation in 1669. Is it possible that the existence of slavery determined the choice of the words "cruel and unusual"? The phrase appears regularly in slave cases dealing with the all too usual abuses, mutilations, and homicides of slaves and the liability of masters. It is not surprising that these same words have become so crucial to our government as it tries to excuse its own common abuses.

"The Department of Justice," Bellinger explained before the UN Committee Against Torture, "has concluded that customary international law cannot bind the Executive Branch under the Constitution, because it is not federal law." The Bush administration's lawyers, in seeking to protect government officials from criminal liability, have continued to qualify our obligations to UNCAT, binding us to a narrow but highly malleable history of prohibited acts. While using the adjectives "cruel," "unusual," and "inhumane" to describe illegal conduct, they nevertheless define these words not according to their usage in international law but according to their ever-shifting interpretations within the United States. The one word that they neither use nor delimit is "degrading," which would render illegal the ritual humiliations of those in custody, the very procedures for which UNCAT had condemned the United States.

The punitive and dehumanizing practices in prisons at home and abroad stigmatize the detained. Their degradation confirms the substandard that prisoners are assumed to be. What do prisoners, "security detainees," and "illegal enemy combatants" in U.S. custody have in common? They are all bodies. Few are granted minds. The unspoken assumption is that prisoners are not persons. Or at best, they are a different kind of person: so dehumanized that the Eighth Amendment no longer applies.

The naked pyramid of flesh at Abu Ghraib, the kneeling and shackled bodies, blindfolded by blacked-out goggles and hooded at Guantánamo, sanction degradation.

And when our government refuses to recognize that "cruel, inhuman, and degrading" treatment has a precise meaning, when our courts deliberately and knowingly continue to ignore obvious violations of human dignity and worth, such cruel and unusual treatment becomes protected in law. In a penal system that has become instrumental in managing the dispossessed, the unfit, and the dishonored, legalistic phrases such as "minimal civilized measure of life's necessities" and the "basic necessities of human life" prompt us to reconsider the meaning of "human."

On June 10, 2006, three detainees at Guantánamo committed suicide. Their law-

yers said that the men had hanged themselves in despair. But perhaps Rear Admi-
ral Harry Harris, the camp commander,
grasped the nature of their resistance. After
he accused them of having "no regard for
life, either ours or their own," he declared,
"I believe this was not an act of desperation,
but an act of asymmetrical warfare waged
against us."

The obscenity of his remark requires
no comment. But Harris perhaps understood that the inmates had fought against
legal incapacitation, making visible what
the law had masked. In their hanging, they
returned to the barbaric punishments that
the law in its enlightenment claims to have
surpassed. They returned to the cruelties of
old in order to testify to the continuation
of these cruelties in more "humane" forms
in a politer time.

# NOTES

PAGE

5    *now-famous "torture memos"*    The *New York
     Times* guide to the memos is available at http://
     www.nytimes.com/ref/international/24MEMO-
     GUIDE.html. The best edition of the torture
     memos, as well as the full texts of the legal memo-
     randa that sought to redefine what constituted
     torture—what Anthony Lewis in his superb in-
     troduction called "an extraordinary paper trail
     to moral and political disaster"—is *The Torture
     Papers: The Road to Abu Ghraib*, eds. Karen J.
     Greenberg and Joshua L. Dratel (Cambridge:
     Cambridge University Press, 2005): 172–218
     and 241–86. See also Jeremy Waldron, "Torture
     and Positive Law: Jurisprudence for the White
     House," *Columbia Law Review*, vol. 105, no. 6
     (October 2005): 1681–1750; Mark Danner, *Tor-
     ture and Truth: America, Abu Ghraib, and the*

*War on Terror* (New York: New York Review of Books, 2004); and Sanford Levinson, ed., *Torture: The Debate* (New York: Oxford University Press, 2004).

6    *American colonists*    For a still unsurpassed analysis of the adaptation of the clause to the exigencies of colonial America, see Anthony F. Granucci's "Nor Cruel and Unusual Punishments Inflicted: The Original Meaning," *California Law Review* 57 (1969):839–865.

15   *former slaves as potential criminals*    Alfred Avins, ed., *The Reconstruction Amendments' Debates* (Richmond: Virginia Commission on Constitutional Government, 1967), 258. As David M. Oshinsky argues in *"Worse Than Slavery": Parchman Farm and the Ordeal of Jim Crow Justice* (New York: Free Press, 1996), the post-emancipation criminal code was thus established as a vehicle of racial subordination. See also Alex Lichtenstein, *Twice the Work of Free Labor: The Political Economy of Convict Labor in the New South* (London: Verso, 1996). For a comprehensive discussion of imprisonment as crucial to the American political order, see Scott Christianson's *With Liberty for Some: 500 Years of Imprisonment in America* (Boston: Northeastern University Press, 1998). For a detailed analysis of the calculated evasive-

ness of slave law, specifically in terms of the *Code Noir* of the French Caribbean, see Joan [Colin] Dayan, *Haiti, History, and the Gods* (Berkeley and London: University of California Press, 1995, 1998): 199–212; and for the South, see Thomas D. Morris, *Southern Slavery and the Law: 1619–1860* (Chapel Hill and London: University of North Carolina Press, 1996).

16  *prisoners' rights movement*    See Malcolm M. Feeley and Edward L. Rubin, *Judicial Policy Making and the Modern State: How the Courts Reformed America's Prisons* (Cambridge: Cambridge University Press, 1998).

23  *reinstated capital punishment*    Nevertheless, the court held in *Atkins v. Virginia* (2002) and *Roper v. Simmons* (2005) that it is cruel and unusual to execute juveniles or mentally retarded persons.

23  *a series of cases*    *Estelle v. Gamble* (1976), *Rhodes v. Chapman* (1981), *Whitley v. Albers* (1986), *Wilson v. Seiter* (1991), *Hudson v. McMillian* (1992), *Helling v. McKinney* (1993), and *Farmer v. Brennan* (1994).

46  *Lewis v. Casey*    For a fuller discussion of this case, as well as the Supreme Court's return to an anachronistic and mandatory deprivation of rights, privileges, and capacities, see Joan [Colin] Dayan, "Held in the Body of the State," *History,*

*Memory, and the Law,* eds. Austin Sarat and Thomas R. Kearns (Ann Arbor: The University of Michigan Press, 1999), 183–249, and "Legal Slaves and Civil Bodies," *Materializing Democracy*, eds. Russ Castronovo and Dana Nelson (Durham and London: Duke University Press, 2002). For the best analysis of civil death, its history, and its strange staying power, see Kim Lane Scheppele, "Facing Facts in Legal Interpretation," *Representations* (Spring 1990): 42–77.

48   *dissenting justices*   See *Jones v. North Carolina Prisoners Union* (1977, Marshall dissenting, joined by Brennan); *Meachum v. Fano* (1976, Stevens dissenting, joined by Brennan and Marshall); and *Lewis v. Casey* (1996, Stevens dissenting).

54   *super-maximum prison*   See Lorna Rhodes, *Total Confinement: Madness and Reason in the Maximum Security Prison* (Berkeley: University of California Press, 2004); Dayan, "Legal Slaves and Civil Bodies"; Dayan, "Ruses of Beneficence and Rituals of Exclusion," http://www.louisville.edu/journal/workplace/issue6/dayan.html; Dayan, "Servile Law," in Eduardo Cadava and Aaron Levy, eds., *Cities without Citizens* (Philadelphia: Slought Foundation, 2003), 99; Craig Haney, "Infamous Punishment: The Psychological Consequences of Isolation" (National Prison Project, ACLU, Spring

1993); Craig Haney and Mona Lynch, "Regulating Prisons of the Future: a Psychological Analysis of Super-max and Solitary Confinement," *New York University Review of Law & Social Change,* vol. xxiii, no. 4 (1977); James Robertson, "Houses of the Dead: Warehouse Prisons, Paradigm Change, and the Supreme Court,"*Houston Law Review,* 34 (1997); Jamie Fellner and Joanne Mariner, *Cold Storage: Super-Maximum Security Confinement in Indiana* (New York: Human Rights Watch, 1997); Jamie Fellner, *Red Onion State Prison: Super-Maximum Security Confinement in Virginia* (New York: Human Rights Watch, April 1999).

56  *prisoners are classified*    For the most acute analysis of penology based on "status," see Scott N. Tachiki, "Indeterminate Sentences in Supermax Prisons Based Upon Alleged Gang Affiliations: A Reexamination of Procedural Protection and a Proposal for Greater Procedural Requirements," *California Law Review,* July 1995: 1117–1148. See also Elizabeth Vasiliades, "Solitary Confinement and International Human Rights: Why the U.S. Prison System Fails Global Standards,"*American University International Law Review,* 21 (2005): 71–99.

65  UNCAT    The text can be found at http://www.unhchr.ch/html/menu3/b/h_cat39.htm.

66 *Amnesty International briefing*    The text can be
found at http://web.amnesty.org/library/index/
engamr510562000.

66 *international standards*    The text of the Geneva
Conventions can be found at http://www.unhchr
.ch/html/menu3/b/91.htm. As for the International Covenant on Civil and Political Rights, the
U.S. ratified it in 1992 but with reservations. See
the U.S. report at http://dosfan.lib.uic.edu/erc/
law/Covenant94/Specific_Articles/07.html.

67 *Detainee Treatment Act*    The text can be found
at http://jurist.law.pitt.edu/gazette/2005/12/
detainee-treatment-act-of-2005-white.php.

69 *Graham-Levin Amendment*    See Alfred McCoy,
"Why the McCain Torture Ban Won't Work: The
Bush Legacy of Legalized Torture," *TomDispatch*
(February 8, 2006), and David Cole, "Why the
Court Said No," *The New York Review of Books,*
August 10, 2006: 41–43. To turn torture into a
matter for technical, legalistic discussion is to
continue a longstanding national tradition. See
Alfred W. McCoy, *A Question of Torture: CIA In-
terrogation from the Cold War to the War on Terror*
(New York: Henry Holt and Company, 2006) and
David Cole, *Enemy Aliens: Double Standards and
Constitutional Freedoms in the War on Terrorism*
(New York and London: The New Press, 2003).

73  *devastating report*    The text can be found at
    http://www.ohchr.org/english/bodies/chr/docs/
    62chr/E.CN.4.2006.120.pdf.

75  *appearance before the committee*    The commit-
    tee's questions and Bellinger's written responses
    can be found at http://www.state.gov/g/drl/
    rls/68554.htm. The U.S. presentations to the com-
    mittee can be found at http://www.usmission.ch/
    Press2006/U.S.PresentationtotheCAT.html. The
    committee's findings, formally released on May
    19, 2006, can be found at http://www.ohchr.org/
    english/bodies/cat/docs/AdvanceVersions/CAT
    .C.USA.CO.2.pdf.

77  *ACLU report*    The text can be found at http://
    www.aclu.org/safefree/torture/25354pub2006
    0427.html. See also Center for Constitutional
    Rights, "Report on Torture and Cruel, Inhuman,
    and Degrading Treatment of Prisoners at Guan-
    tánamo Bay, Cuba" (July 10, 2006), available
    at http://www.ccr-ny.org/torturereport; Human
    Rights Watch, "Supplemental Submission to
    the Committee Against Torture," http://hrw
    .org/english/docs/2006/05/04/usdom13316
    .htm. In July, the UN Human Rights Committee
    also condemned the United States for failing
    to meet its human-rights obligations at home
    and abroad. See http://www.ohchr.org/english/

bodies/hrc/docs/AdvanceDocs/CCPR.C.USA
.CO.pdf. Amnesty International's report, *United States of America: Updated Briefing to the Human Rights Committee on the Implementation of the International Covenant on Civil and Political Rights*, can be found at http://web.amnesty.org/library/index/engamr511112006.

83   *Levin memorandum*    The text can be found at http://www.usdoj.gov/olc/dagmemo.pdf. David Luban, in "Liberalism, Torture, and the Ticking Bomb," *Virginia Law Review,* Vol. 91 (October 2005): 1457, explains how "the Levin memo represents the minimum possible cosmetic emendation of the Bybee memo."

90   *ritual humiliations*    In *Harsh Justice: Criminal Punishment and the Widening Divide between America and Europe* (Oxford: Oxford University Press, 2003), James Q. Whitman focuses on *degradation* as key to the singular harshness of punishment in the United States

92   *asymmetrical warfare*    U.S. Department of Defense, "Three Guantánamo Bay Detainees Die of Apparent Suicide," at http://www.defenselink.mil/news/Jun2006/20060610_5379.html.

# BOSTON REVIEW BOOKS

Boston Review Books are accessible, short books that take ideas seriously. They are animated by hope, committed to equality, and convinced that the imagination eludes political categories. The editors aim to establish a public space in which people can loosen the hold of conventional preconceptions and start to reason together across the lines others are so busily drawing.

THE END OF THE WILD   Stephen M. Meyer

GOD AND THE WELFARE STATE   Lew Daly

MAKING AID WORK   Abhijit Vinayak Banerjee

THE STORY OF CRUEL AND UNUSUAL   Colin Dayan

Printed in the United States
by Baker & Taylor Publisher Services